Masterpieces: Artists and Their Works

Rembrandt

by Xavier Niz

T13209

Consultant:
Joan Lingen, Ph.D.
Professor of Art History
Clarke College
Dubuque, Iowa

Bridgestone Books
an imprint of Capstone Press
Mankato, Minnesota

Bridgestone Books are published by Capstone Press
151 Good Counsel Drive, P.O. Box 669, Mankato, Minnesota 56002.
http://www.capstone-press.com

Library of Congress Cataloging-in-Publication Data
Niz, Xavier.
    Rembrandt / by Xavier Niz.
    p. cm.—(Masterpieces: artists and their works)
    Summary: Discusses the life, works, and lasting influence of Rembrandt.
    Includes bibliographical references and index.
    ISBN 0-7368-2230-5 (hardcover)
    1. Rembrandt Harmenszoon van Rijn, 1606–1669—Juvenile literature. 2. Artists—
Netherlands—Biography—Juvenile literature. [1. Rembrandt Harmenszoon van Rijn,
1606–1669. 2. Artists. 3. Painting, Dutch.] I. Title. II. Series.
    N6953.R4 N59 2004
    759.9492—dc21   2003000066

Editorial Credits

Blake Hoena, editor; Heather Kindseth, series designer; Juliette Peters, book designer;
    Alta Schaffer, photo researcher; Karen Risch, product planning editor

Photo Credits

1 2 3 4 5 6 08 07 06 05 04 03

Table of Contents

Rembrandt van Rijn 5
Young Rembrandt 7
Chiaroscuro 9
Anatomy Lessons 11
Amsterdam 13
Etchings 15
The Night Watch 17
Later Years 19
Rembrandt's Fame 21

Important Dates 22
Words to Know 23
Read More 23
Useful Addresses 24
Internet Sites 24
Index 24

In *Storm on the Sea of Galilee*, Rembrandt used light to show the sailors' struggle against the storm's crashing waves.

4

Rembrandt van Rijn

Rembrandt van Rijn (1606–1669) is a famous Dutch painter. He often painted portraits and scenes from the Bible, such as *Belshazzar's Feast* (shown on cover). Rembrandt is famous for his use of shading. He used light and shadow to paint lifelike pictures and exciting scenes.

In the 1600s, artists made people look perfect in their portraits. Artists painted people with smooth skin and made them look better than they did in life. But Rembrandt chose to paint people just as he saw them. In his paintings, he used light and shadows to show peoples' wrinkles and age.

Most artists painted people sitting still in portraits. Rembrandt liked to show action in his work. He painted doctors looking at a dead body. He painted soldiers getting ready for battle. Rembrandt wanted his paintings to be exciting.

In *The Blinding of Samson*, Samson's (bottom center) toes and fists
are curled in pain and anger. Rembrandt used body gestures to
show what Samson is feeling as he is being attacked.

Young Rembrandt

Rembrandt was born July 15, 1606, in Leiden, Netherlands. As a boy, he was not interested in his school studies. He liked to draw. He often drew his family and the windmills near his home.

Rembrandt's father encouraged his son's talent. Around 1621, he sent Rembrandt to be artist Jacob van Swanenburg's apprentice. Swanenburg taught Rembrandt how to make paint and prepare canvases.

After three years, Swanenburg sent Rembrandt to study with Pieter Lastman. Lastman taught Rembrandt the importance of showing people's clothes and actions in art. Clothing could show if a person was rich or poor. Gestures could show if a person was happy, sad, or angry.

In 1625, Rembrandt opened an art studio in Leiden. He painted and sold scenes from the Bible. People also hired him to paint their portraits.

Light shines down on the painter's work in *Artist in His Studio*.
Rembrandt used light to show the importance of the painter's work.

Chiaroscuro

Rembrandt worked with light in his art. He would draw his father wearing fancy clothes and paint his mother doing chores. In these works, Rembrandt concentrated on the light shining on his parents. He used the light to show the details of their faces. Details helped show his parents' expressions.

While in Leiden, Rembrandt met a group of artists from Utrecht, Netherlands. These artists worked with a new art style called chiaroscuro. Chiaroscuro used light and shadow to show dramatic scenes. Rembrandt worked with this style in paintings like *Artist in His Studio.*

Rembrandt's skills earned him respect as an artist. Wealthy people hired him to paint their portraits. Art dealers from Amsterdam, Netherlands, bought his drawings.

In 1631, Rembrandt decided to move to Amsterdam. It was a large city where he could find plenty of work.

In *The Anatomy Lesson of Dr. Nicolaes Tulp*, one doctor (top center) holds a piece of paper. The names of the eight doctors are written on the paper.

Anatomy Lessons

In Amsterdam, Dr. Nicolaes Tulp hired Rembrandt. Doctors asked artists to paint portraits of them and their students. Tulp wanted Rembrandt to paint a picture of him studying a dead body with seven other doctors.

Traditionally, artists lined up people in rows for portraits. But Rembrandt painted the doctors in a triangle shape. He then could show how the doctors worked with each other.

Rembrandt painted light shining on the doctors' faces. The light shows the lines on their faces. It also helps show the doctors' interest in Tulp's work.

The Anatomy Lesson of Dr. Nicolaes Tulp made Rembrandt a popular portrait painter. Tulp and the seven doctors were happy with his work. Other doctors hired Rembrandt to make similar paintings.

In *Saskia as Flora,* Rembrandt had his wife wear fine clothes. He liked to show off his wealth by having Saskia wear expensive clothes and jewelry in her portraits.

Amsterdam

In 1634, Rembrandt married Saskia van Uglenburgh. She was the niece of his art dealer, Hendrick van Uglenburgh.

In the 1630s, Rembrandt was busy with work. Many people wanted him to paint their portraits. He earned a great deal of money selling his paintings, but he quickly spent the money. Rembrandt bought fine clothes, artwork and expensive jewelry.

During this time, Rembrandt had several students helping him. Apprentices mixed paints and sometimes drew the outlines of portraits. Rembrandt then filled in the details of the paintings. With his students' help, Rembrandt could work on several paintings at one time.

When Rembrandt was not working, he looked for new ideas. Amsterdam was a large city. People from all over the world lived there. Rembrandt enjoyed drawing these people and the different clothes they wore. He also visited the countryside and drew landscapes. Rembrandt used many of his sketches to create new works of art.

In *The Little Children Being Brought to Jesus*, parents bring their children to Jesus (center) to be blessed. In this print, light shines from Jesus, brightening the center of the picture.

Etchings

During his life, Rembrandt created many etchings. Etchings are pictures made on a metal plate. The plate is then covered with ink and used to make prints of the picture. Etchings allow artists to quickly make many copies of one drawing.

Before Rembrandt, artists used hatching in etchings. Hatching is a series of parallel lines. Artists shaded a picture with hatching. Rembrandt thought hatching limited the amount of detail he could show. Instead, he used his etching tool like a pencil. He drew lines of different thickness to shade and add detail to his work.

Rembrandt's etchings gained him even more fame. Rich people in Amsterdam bought copies of his prints.

In 1641, Rembrandt's son, Titus, was born. Soon after, Saskia became ill and died. Saddened, Rembrandt spent most of his time working on paintings and etchings.

In the center of *The Night Watch*, Captain Cocq talks to one of his soldiers. A light shines on them, showing that they are important. The other soldiers are in shadow.

The Night Watch

In 1642, Captain Frans Banning Cocq hired Rembrandt. He wanted Rembrandt to paint a life-sized painting of him and his soldiers. Rembrandt worked on this painting day and night for one year. It showed the soldiers in action. They look as if they might be getting ready for battle. Rembrandt thought the painting would look lifelike if the soldiers appeared to be doing something.

Cocq was pleased with the painting, but many of his soldiers were not. They wanted a more traditional portrait. These soldiers were upset that they were not easily seen in the painting. Some of them are standing behind other soldiers. Some soldiers are not completely in the painting.

Today, *The Shooting Company of Captain Frans Banning Cocq* is known as *The Night Watch.* It had become blackened with tobacco smoke over the years. The smoke made people think the painting was of a night scene.

Rembrandt painted *Hendrickje Bathing in a River* in 1655. Many of his later works were self-portraits and paintings of his family.

Later Years

In 1649, Rembrandt hired a nurse, Hendrickje Stoffels. She took care of Titus. Rembrandt fell in love with Hendrickje. In 1654, they had a daughter, Cornelia.

In his later years, Rembrandt did not earn enough money to support his family. Few people bought his paintings. He also owed a great deal of money. He had bought many fine clothes, a large house, and a great deal of artwork.

In 1656, Rembrandt sold many of his belongings to pay his debts. He also sold his house. Rembrandt then moved his family to a small house in a poor part of Amsterdam.

In 1660, Titus and Hendrickje opened a small art shop. They sold Rembrandt's work to earn money to support the family.

Rembrandt's last years were sad ones. He was poor. In 1663, Hendrickje died. Five years later, Titus died. On October 4, 1669, Rembrandt died. He was 63.

In *The Syndics of the Clothmakers' Guild,* the men look like they were interrupted during an important meeting. Rembrandt is famous for painting scenes that give a feeling of action.

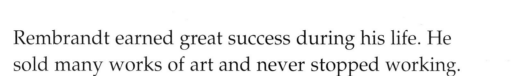

Rembrandt's Fame

Rembrandt earned great success during his life. He sold many works of art and never stopped working. He created more than 600 paintings, 300 etchings, and 1,400 drawings.

Rembrandt's work influenced many artists. His style of etching changed the way prints were made. Artists study his use of light and shadow to learn how to make lifelike paintings.

Today, Rembrandt's artwork is in museums around the world. The Metropolitan Museum of Art in New York has a large collection of his art. The Louvre Museum in Paris, France, and the National Gallery in London, England, also show his work. The most important collection of Rembrandt's art is at the Rijksmuseum in Amsterdam. This museum has many of his famous masterpieces.

Important Dates

1606—Rembrandt is born July 15 in Leiden, Netherlands.

1621—Jacob Swanenburg makes Rembrandt his apprentice.

1624—Rembrandt goes to Amsterdam, Netherlands, to study with Pieter Lastman.

1625—Rembrandt opens an art studio in Leiden.

1629—Rembrandt paints *Artist in His Studio.*

1631—Rembrandt moves to Amsterdam.

1632—Rembrandt paints *The Anatomy Lesson of Dr. Nicolaes Tulp.*

1634—Rembrandt marries Saskia van Uglenburgh; he paints *Saskia as Flora.*

1641—Rembrandt's son, Titus, is born.

1642—Saskia dies; Rembrandt paints *The Night Watch.*

1649—Hendrickje Stoffels becomes Titus' nurse.

1654—Rembrandt's daughter, Cornelia, is born.

1656—Rembrandt sells his house and many of his belongings to pay his debts.

1662—Rembrandt paints *The Syndics of the Clothmakers' Guild.*

1669—Rembrandt dies October 4 in Amsterdam.

Words to Know

anatomy (uh-NAT-uh-mee)—the study of the human body
apprentice (uh-PREN-tiss)—someone who learns a trade or craft by working with a skilled person
canvas (KAN-vuhss)—a cloth surface for painting
chiaroscuro (kee-ar-uh-SKYUR-oh)—an art style using light and shadow to create a dramatic scene
debt (DET)—money that a person owes
etching (ECH-ing)—a picture created on a metal plate; artists use etchings to make prints of pictures.
expression (ek-SPRESH-uhn)—the act of showing feelings
gesture (JESS-chur)—an action that shows a person's feelings
landscape (LAND-skape)—a painting or drawing of an outdoor scene
portrait (POR-trit)—a drawing or painting of a person

Read More

Richardson, Joy. *Looking at Shadow in Art.* How to Look at Art. Milwaukee, Wis: Gareth Stevens, 2000.
Woodhouse, Jayne. *Rembrandt van Rijn.* The Life and Work of. Chicago: Heinemann Library, 2002.

Useful Addresses

Boston Museum of Fine Arts
Avenue of the Arts
465 Huntington Avenue
Boston, MA 02115

Metropolitan Museum of Art
1000 Fifth Avenue
   at 82nd Street
New York, NY 10028-0198

Internet Sites

Do you want to find out more about Rembrandt?
Let FactHound, our fact-finding hound dog,
do the research for you.

Here's how:
1) Visit *http://www.facthound.com*.
2) Type in the **BOOK ID** number: **0736822305**.
3) Click on **FETCH IT**.

FactHound will fetch Internet sites picked by our editors just for you!

Index

*Anatomy Lesson of Dr. Nicolaes
   Tulp, The*, 10, 11
apprentice, 7, 13
Bible scene, 4, 5, 6, 7, 14
chiaroscuro, 9
clothing, 7, 9, 12, 13, 19

drawing, 9, 13, 15, 21
etching, 14, 15, 21
gesture, 6, 7
light, 4, 5, 8, 9, 11, 14, 16, 21
Night Watch, The, 16, 17
portrait, 5, 7, 9, 11, 12, 13, 17, 18